Walking In My Father's SHOES

(life is just a looking glass)

aj houston

copyright © 2011 ajhouston
all rights reserved

Not Just Alphabets Publishing

Fort Worth, Texas

All Not Just Alphabets Publishing titles, AJ Houston, wordart, imprints and lines distributed are available at special quantity discounts for bulk purchases for sales promotion, fund raising, premiums, educational, institutional and library use.

Copyright © 2002 - 2015 by AJ Houston. All rights reserved.

No part of this work may be reproduced or transmitted in any form or by any means, electronic or mechanical, including photocopying and recording, or by any information storage retrieval system without the prior written permission of A.J. Houston or Not Just Alphabets unless such copying is expressly permitted by federal copyright law. Email notjustalphabets@gmail.com address for Permission.

Printed in the U. S. A.

Not Just Alphabets Publishing

Library of Congress Catalog Card Number:

ISBN: 978-0-9963129-5-0

October 7, 1928 - September 26, 2001

Growing up every night I prayed I wouldn't grow up and be like my father, now every night I pray my sons and daughters will pray they don't grow to be like me...
Parenting isn't easy and good parents are not often liked by their children until they grow to become parents...Thank you daddy for the straightening... I am a better man for it...

R.I.P. (Jimmie Jay Houston I)

Foreword:

We live in a time where the family is a battle field and fathers are missing in action on a continued basis. The media screams at hearts frequencies of dead beat dads, son's and daughter's raising themselves, abandoned mother's and the structure of the family has forever changed for the worse. My story is completely different my father was there always, loving, cursing, drinking on the weekends and working every day to provide for his seeds. A true living example of due diligence. He talked of his childhood without a father, but never told us of the dreams and aspirations he had growing up.

It could be he was born in a time where few men could attain their dreams or through time he understood what his father's role should have been, if he had only chosen to stay. I'm guessing, he swallowed his dreams at the birth of his first child, understanding that he would never leave like his father. His words were rough, friends we weren't; but a father he was. I even told myself time and time again if I ever have children I would never be like him. Those were the beliefs I held until the day my daughter walked this great planet.

Every day it was as though my feet were being molded to walk in his shoes. Not the same pair, just a matter of speaking. On that day something in my mind clicked and all the lessons he taught me I never knew existed, blossomed in vivid color. I was now a father. So proud to be there and held her close because she meant everything. It was a new awareness to acknowledge she was depending on me, just as I was on him. There is truly a daily doses of medicine needed in fatherhood. The lessons he gave me were easily recalled because he made them tangible in his daily walk. He had a way of detailing life sometimes using a language only sailors and marines could get away with. These conversations prepared me for those times when love broke into tiny shards of memories, and my daughters were just memories and access to their hugs, tears and kisses were just memories. He said be a man when everything falls apart, hold your head high when nothing is going your way... that's life.

We will at times seem broken and mistakes will be made. When we make mistakes it means you are trying, remember always nothing beats a failure but a try. Every day now, I look down at my shoes and conclude maybe it would be a better fit if the title was Walking In My Father's Feet because shoes can be removed or out grown. Maybe my toes will never reach the edge, so I stumble around in galoshes but no matter what the results every day I resemble him.

My prayer has changed completely now; every night I pray my daughter's and son's will pray, they won't grow up to be like me. Although I have yet to reach my full potential and that is a lesson I hope they learn. Perfection, not even close, it seems only yesterday I learned to spell it correctly. I only wish and strive to be the best me possible and in the process write the Truth's I see, give all the love I have and the role of being a father remains a work in progress. I am still struggling to tie the laces correctly and Walk In My Father's Shoes.

Introduction

Penny loafers; yeah, penny loafers. I think that was the first pair of shoes I owned I mentally can recall were just Sunday shoes. Not everybody can say they were blessed to understand how the foundations set around Sunday mornings created a true precedence of enlightened thought or spirituality. We must become or adhere to some reasonable facsimile of being able to let go of the prejudices of yesterday in order to live our dreams to their fullest. The title "Walking In My Father's Shoes" comes from the idea, if people can be called different names by those who merely are associates and other names by relatives and loved ones: such as... Phillip at home goes by Boo, his friends call him Phil, but he would rather be called Michael. Can we all be narrow minded enough to believe that one Omnipotent God could only have one name, spoken in one language in this multicultural society. If I believe in one God and profess to be a Christian, do the words given me to write sway your judgment of my belief.

Every day I wear my Father's Shoes whether they are penny loafers, tennis shoes, house shoes, plain socks or barefoot. It is not a style of dress, it is embedded in my heart, my spirit, in my mind and in my soul. I am always fully dressed in the foundational truths taught me in early childhood, learned by mistakes made in my adolescent years and anchored in my bones as an adult. Maybe, just maybe, Sunday in my mind could also be my Mondays, Tuesdays, Wednesdays through

life is just a looking glass

Saturdays and begin again every week the same. I am awe struck every time I re-read something my pen wrote-not that I didn't help in the process; but, where did it all come from? That is the question I always ask myself, and no I did not reply.

I thought maybe if I titled the book with a strong mental reference of something positive for myself and the readers, we could open mindedly understand as poets and lovers of poetry, words really do matter. Sometimes we must phrase a piece in a way those not in this circle of conscious thought could grasp the reality of it. We live in a society filled with century old prejudices and standard good old boy practices and they are still common in the work and city place, so my opinion on the matter may seem foreign to you but search for the truth in it.

To truly write elixirs with healing herbs and spices, one must first face the truth head on, then move toward unity of thought. The battle is always won by those with a clear conscience and focused on the best possible solution to the problem or dilemma. We, as a people have lost the cohesiveness to bind together, to breathe together, to band together not just for a common reactionary cause, but to better human kind as a whole. Look back at all the historical inventions that were created by minorities. America's daily existence evolves around those inventions, although unsaid and undocumented in our historically unspeakable past.

Once again the burden weighs heavy like thousands of shackles welded together in the underbelly of slave ships for us to mend this broken society. This resurrection of new poetic performers (slam poets) are filled with verses kind and unkind to our present plight in this new millennium. I believe in the power of the pen. I believe words can heal a broken man or woman. I believe words can teach our youth a new way of rapping truths, I believe in love and I believe poetry has a place higher than the smoky clubs and small closeted rooms in which these spoken word venues are usually held. I believe in life.

So, with my "Father's Shoes" mentality and my bundled beliefs in the American institution, I'll step outside the realm of normal possibilities wearing my gear like an earned badge of courage placed high upon my chest. Speaking words of inspiration, of pain, of healing and of faith, truly believing time will change our lowly standings in this new society. Continuing to write with my last breath, write until my last pen strokes the pages of consciousness, making eyes open wide… as the ink yells to the top of your thoughts; "You Are Here!". Welcome to "Walking In My Father's Shoes".

life is just a looking glass

I Stand in Respect, and in Awe

Proud to pass on the days greeting

with the introduction

I am **AJ Houston son** of

Jimmie Jay Houston

To: **my Father**

(R.I.P.)

Table of Contents

I	14
Refrigerate After Opening	17
Now	21
Warning	24
Sunday Shoes	26
Traffic Cop	31
Did We Miss The Glory	35
N R Out	39
Do You Get My Point	40
For A Friend	43
What About The Children	49
A Strange Encounter	50
Filling Shoes	51
Closet's	53
Remembering Love	56
A Child's Place	59
Searching	63
The Question	67
More Than Poetry	70
Afraid Of Change	75
Write Me A Sunset	77
My Wish	82
Short I	84
Missing Years	85
Spirits	89
Sirens	93

life is just a looking glass

Hoodwinked	97
Miracles	100
Old Souls	102
The Passer By	105
Political Piece	106
On The Sea Shore	110
Spilled Ink	113
Erasing The M's	114
Choice	116
The Declaration of Indecision	121
Redemption (For Tookie Williams)	124
Untitled	128
I Pardoned America	129
Word Warrior	133
More	136
Passion For Pain	139
True Love	143
Why Me	146
The Voices Of Angels (short)	150
The Voices of Angels	151
Purpose	156
Things Father's	160
Product Page	167
Acknowledgements	168
Author Bio	169
Contact & Booking Information	170

all poems are the property of AJ Houston and Not Just Alphabets all rights reserved

life is just a looking glass

yesterday,

I read the writing on the wall

today

I remembered

it was I who placed it there

Walking In My Father's Shoes

I

when I speak of I

it's strictly personal

the days that have passed

are irreversible

I have to look and see

if I can be

The best me

that will in turn

create a better we

when I wade through the moments

viewing my past wrongs

all apologies begin to sound like

the same old song

knowing in my mind this pain

will never last too long

as I look back at the things

I've made it through

I wonder how my heart

could be ready for a brand new start

so soon after you

if it were possible to take

and remake yourself

life is just a looking glass

and build new will

I think I upgraded my old self

then traded what was left

as far as flesh and built me

brand new out of steel

so I now stand here as strong as ever

eyes blinking

constantly thinking

I could still become much better

as I search myself for myself

because one day I know I'll be

the end result

life's test is for

a stronger and more fortified me

when I look in the mirror

seeing I much clearer

than the view

has ever been before

I know if I need to

I can just reach through

the surface of me

to the very core

from there I rise

Walking In My Father's Shoes

like a Phoenix to soar

high above all we think

to be visible

making day to day existence

more livable

when I speak of I

it's truly personal

although this love we give

and daily life we live

is irreversible

so whenever I say I

I just be

pure energy

for the inner me

to become one

with the poet you see

life is just a looking glass

Refrigerate After Opening

(sing) somewhere over the rainbow, way up high

I believe everybody has a favorite song

that touches them to the core of their emotions

the opening line to one of my favorite songs is

"Somewhere Over The Rainbow"

but you see in Oz there was a problem

you had four people searching for the wizard

asking for those things already possessed.

a heart, some courage, a home and a brain

this ain't Oz

but we are still having the same problems

in this new millennium

we have poets and rappers still searching for truth

so often we get caught up in the glamour of success

never seeing the gladiators

the warriors it took get there

how many times have you purchased an item

only to have it go bad before you were ready to enjoy it

at that precise moment

you noticed it came with a warning

you just failed to see it initially

have any of you ever noticed

how everything comes with a label

comes with a warning

in everyday life something

as simple as a loaf of bread

comes with an unwritten label

once opened, you know you must re-apply the tie

keep it in a cool dry place or it will go bad

all dairy products including milk and ice cream

must be kept in their perspective places

wouldn't you think the same principles

would apply to our dreams

can you imagine Michael Jordan

the one with six NBA Championships

five M. V. P. Awards

nine scoring titles

you know… the NIKE guy

can you imagine Michael Jordan

being cut from a basketball team

he knew in his heart

that is what he was purposed to do

that evening when he arrived home

he took his basketball, and put it on the top shelf

life is just a looking glass

in the refrigerator

because he read the warnings on the label

his parents didn't understand

why every time they opened the refrigerator

there lay this basketball on the top shelf

you see, eventually they understood

he was keeping it fresh like fruit

until it became ripe

Bill Gates, you know Microsoft

the guy that was the richest man in the would

he must have also read the labels

read the warnings

when he left Harvard with this dream in his hands

his parents and friends didn't understand

while all the nay sayers were so eager

to dispel his inventions

they didn't have a clue

why he kept this large refrigerator in his garage

he was keeping those dreams stored

until it became time to unveil them

as for me - I learned from my predecessors

I take the time to read the labels

and I watch for life's warnings

Walking In My Father's Shoes

as I journey through this life day after day

and go to the places where I say, what I say

these words never come easy

and I will never take them light

I am even a poet on those days

with no stage and no mic

every evening when I get home I take my pen

place it on the top shelf in the refrigerator

so when you get home, stop and look around you

you will find that everything you love

and everything you are emotional about

comes with a warning, this spoken word is no different

truth is... I can only teach you

referencing the things that I've been through

believe me, there is no such thing as make a wish

and hope that it comes true

because every goal you have set

and dream you have, is complete up to you

the most important factor

is in yourself you must have faith

I am not demanding you refrigerate after opening

but you need to keep those dreams

stored in a cool dry place

life is just a looking glass

Now

sometimes while running forward

I move past to look back

and see myself

simultaneously seeing where I'm going

where I've been and how many minutes

this journey has left

even when writing

with pen and paper fighting

there are so many poets

scribing on the same page

every poet you see

happens to be me

presenting a different mind set

when I was a different age

I telepathically receive

so many directives

from so many perspectives

for I have been a poet from birth

I've been writing words

before true language was heard

after breathing my first breath

upon this earth

and now

it's so important

you understand

how these words flow constant

like grains of sand

you never capture

or hold in your hand

because time standing still

was not in the plan

now... I got to drop

these serious verbs on you

you see - this is it - so no

plain words won't do

I need to chisel the metaphors

that have such strong content

once you hear

you'll drop crocodile tears

and believe these words

contain what life was meant

I stand in this moment

with vision clear

aware of the many battles

I fought to get here

life is just a looking glass

with pen blazing furiously

erasing all doubt and all fear

as I unveil the world

from your eyes

you can see what is real

regardless of what I diagnose

you alone choose

the amount - the dose

or how much you wish

to believe or feel

are you able to shake

then awake from this place

mere faith

could never without

these words reveal

you see - I know now

what I only thought I knew

when I carved words into thin air

that were neither black nor blue

Walking In My Father's Shoes

WARNING! WARNING! WARNING!

I wish that was the cry of all the attendees at my thirteenth birthday. Maybe somewhere in the fun, laughter and the eager thoughts of growing up, I would have heard at least one of the voices.

It seems there was so much to look forward to between puberty and manhood; but everything was based on time. Losing so much year after year, goals were lost, thoughts were lost and purpose was lost and found and lost and found and lost again. To the point where I am not sure if the purpose I presently own is mine to keep. Looking back over the years attempting to find some regret but there is nothing to be sorry for. If one thing in my past is changed, then my present would somehow be totally different.

Believe it or not, these are the most gratifying times I can remember. Poetry has a way of revealing you to you or is that me to me. Every sentence scripted on some torn piece of paper bag or a found corner ripped with intentions to keep, displays where time went. All the time I thought I misplaced can be found on the pages of text all around me. It matters not if the poem or story was ever finished. Words, sometimes incomplete sentences as long as they hold some resemblance of truth, I can remember when and why I wrote them.

life is just a looking glass

It is strange how I sometimes find a little boy in this grown man's body, and to think I believed long ago, there was a grown man in the body of a little boy. The goals and dreams held tightly in the grasp of the little boy in me will always be visible close to my heart. With only one slight change. The level of importance of each has been weighed, rated, measured and categorically placed in order of necessity. Today's list is topped with the overwhelming duty to write. Purpose so skillfully renewed I am reminded of that child one and a half years old that must touch everything in order to insure he or she is alive. So I gotta write; not just poetry, every thought, every pain, every ounce of joy and every breath of truth. Write, so that time remains captured on pages, locked in verse, bound by sentences never to be misplaced again.

Walking In My Father's Shoes

Sunday Shoes

I thought I would come to you barefoot

because sometimes it gets too hard to say

when you have on Sunday shoes

everybody knows

it's time to bow your heads and pray

but when they step up in bare feet

may as well loosen your tie

the top button on your shirt

and get real comfortable in your seat

now it's not just time for prayer

I use these words to teach

then they manifest themselves into words that preach

so no seat in this building is out of reach

can I get you all to bow your heads

it's not an attempt to raise the dead

or lay hands to heal some poor soul

that has not yet been fed

I just want to spit

some of the greatest words

life is just a looking glass

the greatest poet ever said

to everything there is a season

and every one has one chance in time

I chose these words for just one reason

I stepped to this mike, for this chance is mine

if I talked of how true equality would never be

you would probably think that thought was deep

if I spoke of how your presence

made love feel so effervescence

would you let me rock you

into your deepest emotional sleep

if I made the metaphysical - physical

then used the equation

that measures both time and space

turned in into out and out into in

replaced every ounce of doubt

you've ever had or embraced

then I took that huge stack of alphabets

you've had cluttering that corner

far back in your mind

and created verse, unrehearsed

Walking In My Father's Shoes

holding the creation captive

and formed words with such power

that would make the seeing blind

then I took history's blessings

and showed you the lessons

this era had never befriend

I would repeat the exact time to the minute

teaching new value you would find placed in it

so you would hold your pride high

as your journey begins

you see in 1947

it was about a quarter after eleven

when pro baseball was first integrated

they chose one player from the Negro league

to embark on this mission

no one knew it was without America's permission

for she loved her sports truly segregated

now this first instance wasn't the fall

of that great white unmovable wall

but we can call it the beginning of the break

for heaven's sake

life is just a looking glass

you all should be saying

preach man preach

for human kind sake we need to be taught

to be better livers of this life

so teach man teach

present day - in the NFL

they would rather pay a brother's bail

so by Sunday morning he'd be out of jail

then he could be the star of the game

the big screen will keep displaying his name

and in the end zone he could dance a jig

to keep old massah happy, like the fiddler did

believe it or not in the NBA

it is the same old way

they would rather find some lawyers to pay

to keep justice at bay

so the brother can play

until his contract goes away

in every game we have our designated sport's hero's

we all would rather overlook

how much we gain by reading books

as the entertainment

value of the tv grows

while we all sat

mindlessly watching

our favorite tv shows

then you wonder why

to everything

there is a season

and just who guarantees

to everyman

his one chance in time

but there be no doubt

to you the reason

I stepped to this mike

for this chance is mine

life is just a looking glass

Traffic Cop

just recently

I found my mind

was so complexed

my thoughts began colliding

and having wrecks

in order to get this bullish to stop

I had to hire me a mental traffic cop

to unclog the streets and alley ways

Memory Lane is always backed up

with lies of yesterdays

boasting Boulevard usually

has too many cars

from hand claps and praise

received from too many bars

you see a traffic cops job is never done

stopping jaywalkers, speeders

and thoughts on the run

then there are those gang thoughts

that just hang thoughts

for no apparent reason

I gotta make these thoughts flow

so everywhere your mind goes

you can see the beauty in each season

and Bold Stroll

started jacking up the toll

because that is where

all the thoughts would be

it became improbable

next to impossible

to find your true identity

so yea

there is a ghetto in my mind

and sometimes there are lines so long

those beggars on Harmony Lane

crowd the streets with too much pain

making it easy to lose your song

it seemed the fast lane

was full of past things

always exceeding the speed limit

at the intersection of Equality Street

and expectations to meet

there were too many collisions in it

Hope Street was blocked off for repairs

where it crossed at Pride

and over at the junk yard on Disregard

it was full of junk thought cars

that no longer had the ability to drive

on the freeways there were no free days

life is just a looking glass

used to be thoughts would just flow

but now there is a registration

they must claim a destination

before the traffic cop would let them go

and usually the last lane

was used as the fast lane

but all the lanes were treated that way

now the traffic cop

made all this non sense stop

and found a place for the children to play

on Sensitivity Street

they lost their ability to feel

from poets spitting jokes

and the shhh that wasn't real

at night when those traffic lights turn green

thoughts that were seldom seen

were still lost wondering in the dark

on my minds movie reel

I could see all those emotions

I used to feel

like they were main lined from my heart

I'm not saying hiring this traffic cop

has truly eased my mind

or made it easier to cease the time

but it did help my thoughts to flow

if your mind

is too complexed

and thoughts are having wrecks

searching for a solution

now you know

(sound of a whistle, whistle, whistle)

I'm the traffic cop

up in this piece

soon we'll be having

brains for lease

blowing conscious holes

in the back of minds

leaving life's in wreck

we got books and cd's for sale

and we don't accept

MasterCard or checks

hey slam master!

get up here

and tell these people

who's next

life is just a looking glass

Did We Miss The Glory

(I conclude, that first we must become one planet, then one people, then one nation)

proud to be an American

is the popular song of the day

on all the transportation we ride

the red - white and blue
symbol of freedom we fly

basking in the glory
of the American way

we are afraid to travel by air
as we used to do

the skyline of New York

the flags that memories mark

you see all these things are new

 I don't want you to think

I'm reading that same old story

but I have to ask

did we miss the glory?

from the signing of the declaration

to proclaiming our emancipation

genetic memories seem always to last

there are no reparations

because there's no more separation

and I'm not just bringing up the past

I'm saddened by this tragedy

but America don't like having me

now what am I supposed to do

death still plagues our communities

there's more drugs than the eye can see

and the prisons are filled with our sons too

all over the world terrorist activities
bombard the lands

at America's first chance

we grabbed freedom lance

so this will never happen again

from the Civil War to Desert Storm

we've lead Americas freedom fight

when we finally get home in red line zones

we can't even sleep for the sirens at night

so, did we miss the glory?

it's not that same old story

but through all this time
nothing's changed

we attempt to be politically correct

and still in this land there's no respect

at least they no longer call us b

by that degrading name

life is just a looking glass

they may treat me like I'm in the fields

but still I'm making dollar bills

while the price of everything is escalating

family now has forgot it's meaning

even children's shows need a lot of screening

not every issue needs debating

has glory found a new definition?

determined by true politicians

I try to go through life on a positive note

you may think I'm blowing smoke

while I try to keep relationships

and America afloat

I need to know did we miss the glory?

I think it is that same old story

that my father's, father's, father

passed down to me

it might be hard to understand

how the thoughts and concepts of one man

can change a people's ideology

but I don't believe we've missed the glory

I'm sure it's still to come

nothing in the past is lost

but we must surly pay the cost

if we value this land and our freedom

freedom has never been free

and it's not just you and me

it's takes so many more

to balance this past full of pain

so before we even taste the glory

we must create a whole new story

So our sons and daughters

will know freedom remains

So did we miss the glory?

We must continue to tell the story

For we still struggle to be free

Because we could loose on only chance

If we don't stop and take a stance

And rebuild our own communities

(I conclude that first, we must become one planet, then one people, then one nation)

life is just a looking glass

N R Out

From as early as I can remember whether family, friend or game related, the one statement I believed always to be true is: *"you have to make a choice, you can only be one or the other - are you in or out?*

After writing for some time, I was left with one truly difficult choice to make... Do I present the whole picture, or just half? So as a writer, especially as a poet, I am obligated to myself and the reader to write from the perspective of being inside and outside, as though I were viewing the whole thing from the middle ground. I don't believe there can be clarity of thought when you can only see through one eye, or have only the left side in clear view. How can I color the perfect rainbow? if my eyes can only see in black and white. So now, I give you back your question - not while balancing on the fence in the middle ground, but as I stand on this soap box made of solid stone... Answer me this: *are you in or out?...*

Do You Get My Point

in life

there are only two ways you can be

either understanding, or understood

if you don't understand me now

I really wish you could

if I tell you something

you understand

there is nothing more

you need to say

but on the other hand

if you tell me something

that is understood

it works the same old way

before we go too far

and there is something

you may have missed

in life, at every turn

there is a lesson to be learned

but so often we resist

if you ask the professionals

nearly every ailment

life is just a looking glass

can be linked

to a form of stress

I am taking out this time

to drop some knowledge in your mind

for understanding makes you blessed

out of all the things we worry about

you know the list is long

the problems that we face each day

we all sing the same old songs

we suffer the misfortune

of thinking the point was clear

when words that were stated plainly

were not the words we wanted to hear

still trying to change the sentence structure

while the sound is in your ear

let's slow this process down

and get right to the core

regardless of what you may think

there are things we can't ignore

in life, we have our ups and downs

conversational trauma's

with misunderstandings abound

when you finally get to the place

you are being understood

but your choice

of words are wrong

that's really not so good

because, words you can't take back

even though you wish you could

so take the time to understand

it is always best to know

being understood is good

but it is really touch and go

you can't always be understanding

nor will you always be understood

so try to get your point across

my suggestion is

taking time to listen

is the way that should

keep us from ever being lost

life is just a looking glass

For A Friend

the other day

after leaving the doctor's office

I received a call from a friend

he told me of everything

he was going through

and I know how easy it is

to get down on yourself

me… after having 5 back surgeries

more than 6 years of doctor visits

and even more therapy

I'm not getting any better

but what he told me

made all my problems

seem so simple

I consistently pray

for family, friends

and everything thing else

but what he told me

hit me so hard

making me know

I needed to get closer to God

because today I need a miracle

not for me, but for a friend

I've been studying the book of Ezekiel

it's my favorite

of all the stories in the bible because

Ezekiel walked with God

Ezekiel talked with God

so when God told him

he needed him

to deliver his message

but in order

for him to understand it

He carved it into a scroll

and demanded he eat it

so he would know

now every day

it becomes more critical

I keep praying for a miracle

life is just a looking glass

as each day passes

my list grows longer

and my heart grows stronger

for a way to stop all this pain

that rains on mankind

in the form of diseases

and natural catastrophes

like cancer, AIDS, tsunami's

hurricanes, earth quakes

and those terrorist that consistently takes

lives that don't belong to them

I pray one day

we could relinquish this pain

so we could live in a world

that almost seems sane

it's gotten too hard to tell

which of these diseases God gave

between which ones are man made

when was the last time

we found a cure for sure

instead of just a way

for those that are sick

to simply endure

someone needs to take a stand

in the intercessory capacity

because this world is too full

of diseases and tragedies

to my father, my Aunt Pat

Giselle, aunt Edith, my brother Chad,

my cousin Michael

and too many more to mention

I call these names aloud

because I need, to get God's attention

right now, I need you to close your eyes

because this is no longer a poem

you are listening to

this is my prayer

and I hope that it's getting through

now I understand, how 40 nights of rain

can make your pain go away

life is just a looking glass

or 3 days

in the belly of the whale

will make your purpose

come back to stay

this life is not compiled

of the years you live

it's measured in minutes

what really matters, is every second

you gotta put your whole heart in it

I could never stand here and tell you

last night - all night

I stayed up

buried my knees in the ground

letting my tears flow down

until I was prayed up

if I possessed a pen that was magic

I could never write words

tragic enough

for you to feel

like he, and all these families do

Walking In My Father's Shoes

if I subtracted

everyone else from this poem

I couldn't write feelings deep enough

for you to just, feel what I'm going through

there are millions questioning the election

looking for answers

our president when asked

about Afghanistan and Iraq

becomes one of the greatest dancers

it would seem to right

if we could just like

spend those same billions

trying to find a cure for cancer

now I'm struggling, to be like Ezekiel

eating the words of each poem

I keep pouring

my life, heart, and soul in

because GOD

today I need a MIRACLE

not for me... but for a FRIEND

life is just a looking glass

What About The Children

if you could speak

anger into space

would it leave without a trace

or remain locked in grimace on ones face

if you could speak peace into being

how would it look to the un seeing

those that are constantly fleeing

from the wars and turmoil

whether it's over gold

dead presidents, or oil

can you see dead alphabets

falling from the skies

from thousands or millions

of lonely hearts, those daily cries

of pain, like blood rain

that stain of souls

we've lost all control.

for a society lost

who really pays the cost

will we cry then, again and again.

my only thought is

what about the children

A Strange Encounter

I met myself the other day

with beard so full

and hair light gray

at first, I didn't believe it so

but I told me things

only I would know

I said, in order to complete

the task at hand

then I grabbed my arm

and took my pen

the words I wrote were

etched in my heart, finish every job

of words you start

for you never know

which will be, the ones

that enlightens

the me you see

and the main thing

you can never forget

they are never

just mere alphabets

life is just a looking glass

Filling Shoes

Historically, I don't know who first coined the phrase, it has been in existence way before my time. Its common use, refers to a pair of shoes fitting someone else's feet, as being the sole requirement for another continuing a job already set in progress. Such as, when President John F. was assassinated, or his brother Robert, the question in bold type was **"who will fill their shoes?"** While in the midst of the battle for the civil liberties for minorities in this country, Martin and Malcolm were both killed in the line of fight; and again the same question came to the forefront, **"who will be able to fill their shoes?"** If that is still not enough, at the retirement ceremony of Kareem, Dr. J, Larry Bird, Wayne Gretzky, Kevin McHale and Michael Jordan, we heard those same sentimental echo's, **"Will there be anyone to ever fill their shoes?"**

We must at some point and time realize, it is never nor will it ever be the shoes. This is not a modern day tale of Cinderella. Until we understand, my favorite phrase of all time which was written by George Clinton, **"you can walk a mile in my shoes, but you can't step a lick in my feet"**, we will never come close to comprehending this filling of shoes dilemma.

We could all wear a pair of Jordan's, whether old or new, and that would not make us have game. We could wear Bo Jangles tap shoes, take tap lessons, but we could never have his creativity or steps. So it is not in the shoes. If our eyes are focused merely on a pair of leftover shoes, we could never see the purpose we were birthed to complete, or rather begin. There is no way someone else's ice skates, basketball shoes, or comfortable walking shoes could make a nation follow you from Selma to Washington, make you MVP of the National Hockey League, or grant you the ability to win six National Basketball Association Championships. So we are stuck in our own feet, searching for our own purpose in this life. We try on many pairs of shoes, some new, some hand me downs, but we still struggle to find our place. I will continue to write, type, speak, sing and use whatever talents I have been endowed with, until I truly etch my place in the society of conscious thinkers.

I am begging you, forget about filling someone else's shoes and just search for a pair that fits your purpose. Then and only then, will you feel true satisfaction in each breath you take and in each heart beat you are blessed to have. Every person you meet, will know that your purpose will not go undone; because, you are putting on your own shoes and placing your best foot forward, one at a time as you greet life with a smile. It is never about the shoes. Greatness is found, in the heart of the person whose biggest fear is: it may only be up to that one individual to get the job done. Never forget, it is not in the shoes, it is in the person who takes the time to put them on one at a time. Although sometimes, afraid of failure, but continues to do his or her best to accomplish purpose.

Closet's

we all embrace for the shock

when someone merely mentions

closet doors opening

hiding the skeletons

we've never seen

it's not a choice, but a necessity

that today, I finally come clean

I've been secretly writing prose

from the day of my birth

dropping verbs like thunderous words

that created the fault lines in the earth

and you think the hurricane was created

from a small spiral in the ocean

you see, I wrote that wind

as I held my pen

while the thought, was just a notion

as you marvel at the shooting stars

that fly so freely across the sky

I wrote those too

they were just for you

when I was sad and didn't cry

and that beautiful sunrise

every morning

that highlights each new day

I made the stencil

and used color pencils

so it will always look that way

do you know how hard it is

to try and draw

the many shapes of the moon

I meticulously take my time

to color between the lines

careful not to have

the wrong shape too soon

I can account for nearly every event

you may consider, an immaculate recovery

because every time I hold my pen

over and over and over again

I write in scientific discoveries

you see, I'm just a poet

plain and simple

with a master's degree

in psychology

using these verbs

to massage your temple

life is just a looking glass

erasing the complexities

of the things we see

showing naturally

true creativity

I birthed nature's beauty

and its disasters

by spilling ink on these pages

then emerged from my closet

to perform on life's stages

it was always believed

an impossibility

through this eternal darkness

I could still write

but the first lines

I ever scribed were

"LET THERE BE LIGHT!"

Remembering Love

(Intro for cd) - "everywhere I go I hear poets, with those sad sad poems, about love gone wrong, and how they've given up on love or men or women. All those who feel, they have been slighted and cheated, or thought they were misguided and beaten. What I'm saying, is don't blame love. We can all sing the same sad songs, but I truly believe - love never fails. Yes, that's what I said, **Love Never Fails!** And you know, just thinking of it, you know the thought of love or just being in love; anyway check this"

when I, yeah... when I, remember love

I remember two pony tails in the seat in front of me

I pull your hair, and act like it wasn't me

when I, when I remember love

I remember, my first kiss by the swing set

in the playground, acting as though

I really didn't like it

when I, when I remember love

I think back to my first touchdown

you were just as excited as I was

and we embrace so tightly after the game

when I, when I remember love

I remember kissing you

life is just a looking glass

before boarding the plane

and promising to write you everyday

as I left to go, and serve my country

when I, when I remember love

I recall, walking the beaches in Spain

the gondoliers in Venice

the beautiful flowers of Amsterdam

the full moon, on the peaks in Switzerland

when I, when I remember love

I can, I can, I can still feel the rush

after receiving the call

having to drive as fast as possible

to the hospital to bear witness

to the miracle of child birth

when I, when I remember love

I remember getting four day passes

dressing in the same colors

riding all the rides at Disney World

and watching the fireworks

in the night sky

as we cruised to the Islands

when I, when I remember love

I see all the faces

that have passed through my life

and not one sad moment appears

when I, when I remember love

I think back to buying my first bowling ball

perfecting my curve

entering my first bowling league

and not being surprised

when we emerged the victors

when I, when I remember love

I remember taking that big chance

at pitch and toss

losing all my money in Vegas

and later you and I

enjoyed the cool strolls

and the bright lights on the strip

So when I, when I

you know when I

remember love

I distinctly

I truly and distinctly

remember You

life is just a looking glass

A Child's Place

I find myself, always going back

back, to my mother's house

that used to be my family's house

before my father passes away

searching for shadowed footsteps

and lost conversations

because now, what I need to know is

what was it back in the day

that made us as children

believe we were safe

before, safety used to be a priority

now this homeland security

doesn't make us feel secure

and mother America constantly demands

more than we could ever give

to date we've lost more than 5000

of our sons and daughters

across the waters - playing in the sand

shipped home in boxes and body bags

wrapped in American flags and dog tags

while their moms and dads

will tell you, this is mass destruction

no weapons needed

in Texas, over 120 of our babies

have been found lifeless

while in the safe custody of CPS

if no charges are filed

I just need some understanding at best

we Americans be like sheep

believing, whoever and whatever they say

downloading lies in constant streams

on this information superhighway

it has gotten so bad, that tragedies

no longer impact me

they seem to occur

so frequently on this rock

but when it comes to our children

we have to find a way to make it stop

while watching the news

I heard a broadcaster

speak of a recent disaster

in a land, that used to be so far away

the problem is, this world

is not as big as it once was

as I listened to the words in English

life is just a looking glass

I could swear

I heard the emotions in Russian

a language I have experienced

but never understood

I couldn't tell the difference

of the alphabets

by looking at them

but I am very much aware

of what pain sounds like

when it comes to our children

earthly origin doesn't matter,

ethnic origin doesn't matter

the only thing that matters

are the children

how can anyone tell

a mother of two

one life, you will definitely lose

how can you tell a mother

it is up to you which one - so choose

what if? you only had

a certain number

of hours and minutes left

to tell your child, you loved them

what if? all that remained

of your life, was 62 hours

what if? you were the parent

standing behind police lines

while marking the end

of your child's life time

but when they left for school this morning

you were sure, they would be just fine

I have never understood how anyone

could sacrifice innocence for political gain

our children are counting on us

to guard them from life's unforeseen strains

and for my son's, I want to be the one

to intercept their pain - no child

no child in this whole wide world

should ever have to ask if in the morning

it will still be raining bombs

or if that stray car is planning to bring us harm

or if some stranger that approaches

is need for true alarm

because a child's place

should always be safe

even away - from his mother's arms

life is just a looking glass

Searching

when I step in the building

I stop and open my mind

while I'm thanking God

for birthing new thought

and searching new thought

everybody else is just mocking time

my sisters are always spitting

and flowing about you hitting

the ultimate prize between their legs

how many breaths did you take

or heartbeats did you count today

given from God, and you didn't have to beg

so you think, these words you spit

you can just hit and quit

because it has this melodic flow

I don't want to alarm you

while others try to charm you

but you need to know

where you're trying to go

don't search for yourself after the piece

or search for yourself during the piece

start searching for yourself

before the piece begins

we can't have these rapid clichés'

repeating and deleting

themselves everyday

like the blind leading the blind

and you're just spitting

while mocking time

like you can't find the words to say

before you start your search

stop and take one deep breath

and say thank you

for this air - of course

why you think you be

just breathing freely

you need to be conscious

of the source

when I first began this mission

of writing with permission

there were some things I had to get past

like the day, I prayed my wife

would have stayed

or that relationship would be my last

but still every day before the sun rises

life is just a looking glass

I have to spit my thanks

you see - I am never marching time

or just patiently standing in line

I rise above the ranks

I have already searched the Everglades

to find the words to say

that will be much colder than before

I have searched the medical Almanac

to find the way, the cure, the facts

now, I be the writer of the cure

I have searched

from the outermost realms of space

too many layers below

the earth's surface

to find if I write - the lines tonight

would I still be in search

of my very own purpose

if one day I arrive at journey's end

would my ink no longer flow

thick but thin

before I search through tomorrow

for my new journey to begin

we ride this vicious circle

at speeds that are irreversible

so between each second

of conscious thought

or free verse we spit

that is stolen or bought

we need to stop and give thanks

for this air - of course

so why you think you just be

breathing freely

you need to be conscious

of the source

when I step in the building

I stop and open my mind

while I am thanking God

for birthing new thought

and searching new thought

everyone else

is just mocking time

life is just a looking glass

The Question

one day, I was asked the question

why I wear black

but I wrote this piece in red

and I bet, sometimes

you don't understand

a word that I have said

if perchance, I broke it down

into its most simplistic form

into words that you have heard

but I'd fear they'd do you harm

but you asked why I write black

but I wrote this piece in red

now - let me slow down

and pronunciate

So you'll understand

just what's being said

I suppose you expect an answer

like all other questions do

so I'll hold my pen

so the west wind

can blow my ancestors through

I am a derivative of the past

Walking In My Father's Shoes

for true knowledge transcends

even if I began at the beginning of me

that is where my ancestors end

if I began to speak the ancient language

like the Kings and Queens, back in the day

it will only leave you pondering

how America, really came to be this way

now you asked, why I write black

but I wrote this piece in red

I filled my pen

with America's sins

of the innocent blood, that's be shed

now the true answer lies

in conversations

our society, is too ashamed

to communicate

like how, Columbus

could be lost in the Bahamas

and still be the founder of the states

or how we could have misplaced our ancestry

because of records that were inept

or why America's history

is so full of blasphemy

life is just a looking glass

and believe me, quiet is truly kept

or how, all those corporate giants

are still functioning

on the inventions of the slaves

and how we use our penal system

as the only intervention

for minority youth that misbehaves

the list could go on much further

but all that was not in the plan

I am told - simple is

what simple does

and simple questions

are usually asked, by a simple man

but sometimes

it takes two hands to hold my pen

for eternal strength

is what I lack

or maybe

I could just get with you later

to try and explain

why I write BLACK

More Than Poetry

I just want to write words

that are different

I don't want to write

just another love poem

I want to write the words

I could actually give

in exchange for your heart

I don't want to write

just another love poem

I want to write one line

one line, that renames

every star in the night

I want to find a word

just one-word, defining both

the dark and the light

I want to speak, and it becomes

the gleam in your eyes

I want to write the words

to that verse, to that song

that makes the steam in your thighs

I want to write the words

every poet, would wish they had wrote

life is just a looking glass

I want to fill the page

with thoughts, so profound

every junkie, would want to

roll up and smoke

I don't want to write

just another love poem

I want to write words

that would make the thunder roll

I want to write words

that would seep, through flesh

into your soul

I want to write words to cure cancer

and all those other bad ass deceases

I want to write so deep on this paper

every blind man could see this

I want to write the love

every person has wished for

but it's been impossible to find

I want to write the words

controlling the essence of time

I want to write words

so simple, they just seem so complex

I want to write words

once you hear them

they will be much better than sex

I don't want to be just another poet

writing just another love poem

I want to write words so soothing

you'll feel no vacation is needed

I want to write the words

when you read them

you feel your life's been completed

I want to write the words

they start making movies about

I want to write that poem

you feel, you can't live without

I want to write words

that will make the sunshine at night

I want to write words

that change your bad disposition

you start enjoying, this new love life

you see, I don't want to write

just another love poem

I want to write words

that bring you

true clarity of thought

life is just a looking glass

I want to write the words

through all of time

even the ancients have sought

I want to write one line

that lets you know

this moment will last

I want to write the words

to fill that void in your mind

making you forget

all of the pain of your past

I want to write the words

deeper than those on the pyramids

those scholars have not interpreted yet

I want to write a poem that feels

better than the kiss

you know you can never forget

I want to write that poem

that every poet

will always wish they had wrote

I want to write the words

so mind altering

we began taking them like dope

I want to write words

that would fascinate

the greatest of minds

throughout both modern

and ancient times

have professors studying

and copying these lines

children will be singing

and repeating these rhymes

those with hearing impairments

will be saying them in sign

and the hardest of hearts

will be listening and crying

you see, I don't want to write

just another love poem

I want to write the words

I could one day give

in exchange for your heart

oh but this...

these are not those

this is just the day

I will start

life is just a looking glass

Afraid of Change

the elections are over

and we all can see

our officials are still the same

we have failed to use our civil liberties

I guess, we are so afraid of change

we all say we vote

but the truth is in the quote

let me pass some words on to the wise

it's treated like a game

but we have failed to rearrange

this so called system, we despise

so I guess for the next couple of years

there will be some griping and some tears

claiming our backs are against the wall

but we treat it like a joke

every time we fail to vote

look like the humble masses

are not so great but small

if you have some words to say

but you did not vote the other day

don't attempt to step into my space

Walking In My Father's Shoes

I can't afford to spend any time

because I believe this country is mine

and I don't want to look you in the face

I don't know a number to quote

on how many have died

for us to have the right to vote

if I did to you it would still be the same

the moment has passed away

Texans could have made history

just the other day

but so many are too afraid to change

we'll put our friendship on hold

don't forget

that you've been told

just get a voter's registration card

and sign your name

because I don't want to hear

the sad songs

you sing into your beer

while you wait

for two more years

Just to show

that you have changed

life is just a looking glass

Write Me A Sunset

a lady friend, came to me the other day

eyes filled with sorrow

she told me of how life had been filling

all her days with darkness

then asked, if I could write her a sunset

immediately, I pulled out my red pen

and began to write in crimson

crimson, like the blood dripping

from hearts shattered and torn

lacking the touch of loves gentleness

needing loves healing powers

crimson stains, like those worn on the faces

of the hundreds of thousands of workers

that are no longer working

for the corporations they help to build

crimson like those days, too hot to run and play

so we just sat in the backyard

letting the evening sky be our entertainment

then I searched to find a pen

with a hue of blue

so deep, it cries oceans

and began to sketch the pain and loneliness

only remembered, when thunder calls your name

and I followed the rain to the end of the rainbow

to recover the smiles

that had somehow lost their way home

you see, I'll write you a sunset

but first I must write the clouds away

and it's not done yet

I closed my eyes to gather

all the strength I could muster

twisted the pens together

until the ink ran orange

then I began to carve into life's canvas

those memories of childhood friends

that couldn't wait until a new day began

and they pledged to be friends till the end

for they possessed no thoughts

of ever growing old

you see, sunsets only meant to them

a new day was about to begin

and every tomorrow, always held the promise

of being so much better than today

then I wrote those giant orange rays

like we used to do in those earlier grades

hoping you would be able

to find your way back to me

Just in case you ever needed me

to write you a sunnier day

in my mind the sunset only means

life is just a looking glass

it is time for the rising of the moon

and this life is way too short

to be quitting too soon

so I guess, it is really different to you

when the day appears too dark

and its only noon

next, I began scurrying to find a pen

the color of love

yeah, love… you know that love

between childhood friends

when no kisses are exchanged

and we didn't hide from the rain

and it was natural to embrace

as we shared each other's pain

all those things that would now seem

to be too strange

I never asked the question

because I didn't need to know the answer

whether it was a pending surgery

sickle cell, HIV or cancer

I knew when I saw her, she had something

she needed to get off her chest

maybe those doctors were discussing

cutting off her breast

or some other sickening ailment

that could make her feel less

Walking In My Father's Shoes

I just wanted her to know

whatever she was going through

if she ever needed me

I so much more needed you

real love, is not

just some mindless affection

used to camouflage

a physical erection

even if she had

to receive weekly chemo

or carry a bag full of pills

we need to get together

combining our prayers

and our wills

making them one

maybe we don't possess the power

to remove or erase

but if you need to talk

I will listen

I just want to remove

the tears from your face

so yes, I'll write you a sunset

but you can never forget

as long as you breathe

no matter how much you bleed

you can give up yet

life is just a looking glass

then I stepped back

to look at the completed picture

all I could think of

was how I could never write

what only God could create

I kept telling my friend

it's never too late

as I looked her in her eyes

I remembered something

I promised myself, long ago

I would never forget

you have always been

more beautiful

than any sunset

My Wish

I've tried hard to recall, what I wished for while sitting at the table blowing out the candles with my eyes closed on my third birthday, but I just can't remember. After so many birthdays, and so many candles blown out, I am still unable to recall, if any of my past wishes came true. Throughout life, we seem to want the simplest things and we choose to phrase them as wishes for whatever reason. Maybe, just out of habit.

I believe wishes come in all shapes and sizes like gradients of gray. It is stated, there are at least two hundred and fifty - six distinguishable shades. But my wish is that I could have the energy, that sudden burst of energy of a three-year-old, when he or she has stayed up way past their bedtime. When they are told it is time to go to bed and they began to cry; I mean cry like they are fully awake, having enough energy to last at least three to four more hours. That is what I wish for. When I am writing or working on something I truly need to finish, and my eyes began to close from the passing of too much time. Work and other meaningful endeavors of the day have drained my usefulness, that is when I want the fruition of my wish to take over.

I want to have that sudden burst of energy, energy enough to write nine more pages of text that is at least eight pages wide, holding my pen with a new born force like the tears of that three-year-old.

life is just a looking glass

Who feels if they close their eyes they may miss something. I do not want one thought to pass unnoticed, or one line to go unwritten. I want tears to flow like rain, giving me the power to keep on writing past the time my body wanted to give up for sleep. My wish is for the need, to continue to scribe conscious metaphors that unearth those feelings hidden behind the lines sleeping eyes could never see. Those thoughts escaping my mind's eye in the tears that are running down my face. So I can catch them, and write them, not letting tired hands skip pass the keys as to miss anything.

If ever I had one wish come true in this life, that would be it. I wish for the mindset of a three-year-old at bedtime, so I will never let sleep overtake my creative senses and continue to produce quality words with the force of automatic tears, giving me renewed energy to continue to write, not missing anything.

Short 1

I

I wish

I could

tell you

how I

truly feel

but somehow

these days

are replaying

like minutes

and these attitudes

are filling seconds

that compile

themselves

into months

of discouragement

so while I

have a clear view

of the sunshine

on this

cloudy day

let me

tell you

I Love You

life is just a looking glass

Missing Years

tears, tears ain't shhh!

when a judge demands that you quit

being a father

I can't explain this pain truly

while relinquishing your parental duties

watching every man that goes through this

eyes fill with water

turning loving fathers into name games

as they attempt to stay sane in this blame game

knowing all the time no amount of money

can make a man be the same thing - as a dad

so you think I don't want to take care of my kids

and you think this shhh happen

because of something I did

just speaking on this subject

makes me feel real bad

I have to pay her more than it takes for me to live

I don't have any more that I can give

so I'm committing crimes for missing

birthdays, yesterdays

school plays and game days

I guess I'm sitting on at least

Walking In My Father's Shoes

ten thousand counts

could somebody tell me what does it take

for me to be a daddy

what does it take for me to be

the father I want to be

just give me the amount

I'm hearing constantly about dead beat dads

it seems it's just a growing fad

but I'm here to tell this shit's getting bad

when you have fathers with this passion you see

years missing inaction ain't the place to be

I just want my children growing up beside me

is that too much to ask

from 3 to 14 those missing years

could never be filled by crying tears

how can you make up for gaps in time

I hear those angry words from step fathers

saying a daddy you ain't so don't bother

so whatever you say today

I've already told them

don't pay you no mind

have you noticed the increase lately

on how many young daughters are having babies

life is just a looking glass

attempting to recapture their daddy's love

that was lost in the past

if you just heard this from me

it doesn't mean nothing

on this poetry stage

huffing and puffing

just find an absent

child support paying father

and just ask

you see, my daughters

already made me a grandfather

when I ask to see them

they make me feel like I'm a land robber

stealing bits and pieces of life

how come didn't nobody tell me

I'd be living in hell to see

my children and F**k it - my ex-wife

now I'm suffering from day horrors

even creeping into my tomorrow's

so you see - sorrow is the only thing I know

the saddest thing

is for the woman you gave your ring

to tell you to pack up your shhh and go

somehow the story of me

they grew up with is slanted, granted

it must be some derivative of the truth

but purposely planted

attempting to make me fill the empty space

on some unwanted fathers list

let's just say perhaps

I did the same

on a quest to slander her perfect name

I'd bet you then

she would be equally pissed

but right now I need help, or longer arms

to reach pass this conclusion

or the illusion

a father is supposed to be like that oak tree

and always stand strong

but to me, it is so confusing

all these fathers are always losing

because a father's true strength

lies in his ability

to raise his own children at home

life is just a looking glass

Spirits

Ummm....Ummm...

I call the ancient spirits of the griots

to hover all the worlds poetry stages

as I open the book of words

unleashing truth, from within these pages

all over the world, poets step behind mics

for entertainment

just attempting to raise the roof

but it becomes sure beauty

when the writer performs his duty

inciting true perception in our youth

I know I am just one miss-step away

from standing with hands out

waiting in some soup line

I am also just one verb away

from a million dollars

for scribing that perfect rhyme

truth be told, this is not a quest for gold

but a search for inspiration

deep within your soul

for the strength to continue to hold

on to warm dreams, when life turns cold

I need the ancient griot's guidance

because I find no peace in silence

Walking In My Father's Shoes

and I'll continue to pray, every single day

I stay anchored in the words I say

so I guess, I'll have to be broke

I will never resort to poetic jokes

or jumping and screaming as mere smoke

to make up for not having the words

to help you cope

making you feel there is so little hope

now all you can do is slang some dope

you will have to know, I love you this much

now every time I touch - my pen

I sacrifice some part of me

I give it to you willingly

so you'll know how strong true love can be

as I offer my all through poetry

true or false, can the truth in verse

create order out of chaos

or do we reach past the facts

to find lies be those tracks

we follow to lands that don't exist

never trying but always believing

this life could be much better than this

if I came here today, and gave you all some seeds

and it were possible to plant wishes

and they grew like trees

but in order to make them grow

life is just a looking glass

you only need to believe

there would be so few left to hold on to

for many would be lost

in the first small breeze - like leaves

so please - I just want you to know

my purpose is to help your thoughts to grow

to rid you of the mind set of I don't know

vanquishing those distraught feelings

when you feel you can't go no more

sometimes, all you really need is a word

sometimes a helping phrase

is all that needs to be heard

to help you get up

and turn that television off

helping you look back and find

past dreams that were lost

telling you to reach deep

because you now know

you are able to pay the cost

I call the spirits of dead poets to rise up

and help me find a solution

because every night, at some open mic

there is no resolution

for those angry words, those tangled verbs

we need a revolution

I don't believe one man, can truly make a stand

and stop this air pollution

it is really hard to cope

when so many poets got jokes

as we consciously battle through this land

so tonight, even if I'm all alone, I'm standing strong

and drawing a line in the sand

I refuse to go out like that

acting as if there is nothing I can do

this poetry is in my bones

so to these words I must stay true

now every night, I gotta write words so tight

in order for you to feel me too

if you are listening for perfection

you won't find it here

because we are all suffering

from one of life's infections

of past failures and short comings

and lacking those things that can help us to be

words of truth create bonds surpassing mere nationalities

so I hope you feel these words

and it is not just the performance you see

Ummm... Ummm...

I call the ancient spirits of the griot's

to hover over all the worlds poetry stages

as I close the book of words

for truth is eternal with in these pages

life is just a looking glass

Sirens

I hear sirens in my life

and no one's even bothered to dial 911

no emergency medical services vehicles

for pain deadened spirits

or murdered dreams lying stiff and unnoticed

by on lookers looking onward

because hope was killed so long ago, rigor mortis set in

and no one has even bothered, to notify the coroner

I hear sirens in my life

from having too much strife

and no time to write - for mind's eye closed tight

for I couldn't stand to listen, to my pen at night

all it would talk about is, how jacked up

we treat each other sometimes

and how I used to snort these poetry lines

to soothe my trouble mind

but they no longer get me, as high as I need to be

to erase life's pains, I see

for we can't truly feel the depth

unless it happens to someone

Walking In My Father's Shoes

in our very own family

it's a shame

walking down the street, seeing babies having babies

walking with babies, so just maybe

my pen will have the solution, to save me

for I could never feel better about this, even if they paid me

these sirens never stop, and I could never drop

the words hard enough, to shake the earth

to wake up all those, who have forgotten

what this life is truly worth

this poetry used to soothe me, as it scribed my destiny

through brail lines, only blind eyes see

for without pen and paper, I could never be

but I've learned to write of sirens

that no longer scream, of broken promises

and broken dreams

no longer leaves battle scars, on inner city wars

while giving hundred year sentences

to black youth behind bars

it seems to rain sometimes, upside down

and we wore clouds like shrouds

in crowed ghetto towns

life is just a looking glass

I thought of calling the medi-vac

to find a way to lift my spirits

but when my mind screams, even then it seems

only my life can hear it

I've spent days tracing life lines, through time

trying to muffle the sound, of hearts breaking

of souls aching, of tears forsaken

there's no time to chill

for too many have lost their will

to live, or ever care

I hear sirens in my life

when no cars are even there

thunder reminds me, of those blunders behind me

when I tried to do so much right

my father told me, all closed eyes ain't sleep

most of the things you love you can never keep

and even the blind has an inner sight

searching for solutions

and for clarity for the mental

I believe it's accidental

this pain in the central part of my brain

so I wonder, if I could use some Clorox

to get out this stain

you see this life keeps

getting the best of me

but I'm not quitting that easily

they will never get the rest of me

I'll use my pen to defend

what is left of me

it seems to rain sometimes

right side up

and I believe this world

is getting tough

because of my dreams

I can't give up

I hear sirens in my life

and no one's even bothered

to dial 9-1-1

I am chasing dreams here tonight

and sometimes I believe

to get rid of this pain

I need to buy a gun

life is just a looking glass

Hoodwinked

Lord, I'm calling because I need your help

I know I can't complete this mission by myself

I keep telling our young if it's not for love

but for hope of wealth

sometimes I spit these words

and they are just for my health

while searching through

the shadows of our recent past

when we were a proud people

having more hope than money

we erased all traces of wearing black faces

and no concept of the word nigger

was ever thought to be funny

now we have rappers and radio commercial spots

dropping n-words like they thought it was hot

no joke could be said or rap be correct

unless you drop the word nigger

like it has some respect

it's a shame that our youth

think that it is so cool

to be the first in the click

to straight flunk out of school

so I guess they chose the proper greeting

when they say - what's up fool

I know my people are suffering from a lack of knowledge

not that bull they are required to study in college

our young boys need to be in the family plan

they've been taught how to procreate

but no classes offered on how to be a man

so - Lord, I'm calling because I need your help

I know I can't complete this mission by myself

I keep telling our young if it's not for love

but for hope of wealth

sometimes I spit these words

and they are just for my health

I've witnessed so many changes in this new society

and we've lost most of our civil liberties

the government has given the FBI the authority

to listen in on conversations, held by you and me

I'm beginning to conclude

we are traveling reverse in time

I have to closer watch your back, and you watch mine

I know you're listening

but you think this is just a simple rhyme

I'll bow my head as I drop this next line

life is just a looking glass

Lord, I'm calling because I need your help

I know I can't complete this mission by myself

I keep telling our young if it's not for love

but for hope of wealth

sometimes I spit these words

and they are just for my health

I'm here to tell you that after all this time

we've been mentally shackled

and economically hoodwinked

while my ancestors were lying in the belly of the beast

I know they wished those ships would sink

with all these games in this new millennium

our children don't even take the time to think

I have to pray sometimes, before I scribe these lines

so often I feel, as though I'm wasting ink

bow your heads and pray with me

oh - Lord, we are calling because I need your help

for we know, we can't

complete this mission by ourselves

we keep telling our young, if it's not for love

but for hope of wealth

sometimes we spit these words

and they are just for our health

Miracles

through all this worlds turmoil,

terrorist attacks,

political deceit and economic woes

I think I may be the only one

who still believes in miracles

yes, I believe in the miraculous

the supernatural, the spectaculous

like parting the seas,

healing the sick, raising the dead

and using a couple of fish

and five loaves of bread

for thousands of hungry listeners to be fed

so I write these words

and sprinkle them like salt

using lyrics like ancient spirits

making lame men walk

because I believe in miracles

I know rivers too, and I know why the cage bird sings

and I know if you can keep your head about you

you too can do miraculous things

it's a shame, so many people stay pissed off

while traveling through life's lessons

life is just a looking glass

missing all the miracles for sometimes

they are hiding in the simplest blessings

this life teaches us way too soon

what we are supposed to do

but sometimes through education

we get lost in the situation

and we are left without a clue

I am always searching for new ways

to inspire young minds

I am always searching through the real

to spark new ideas putting life in new lines

because the best thing we can do for our youth

is infuse this verse with nothing but the truth

it is important we understand

how of little significance we are

one life amongst billions

one earth

amongst countless galaxies of stars

so yes, I still believe in miracles

because I know

that is what it will take

I am forced to write in miracles

to keep sleeping minds awake

Old Souls

sometimes, my soul aches

for I know, I am somehow connected

to old souls, murdered because of their color

whether red, yellow, black or green

murdered for just being

sometimes, my bones ache

from the cracking of necks from old souls

hung from slave trees, if there be such a tree

my heart hurts

from the memories of those fathers

unable to protect their families

from the torture and torment, after being torn apart

unable to prohibit the sale of their offspring

unable to stop the rapping of their wife's

my heart hurts from old pains

lingering in a timeless void

clinging to this earth, like a scab

on a healed wound unwilling to let go

thoughts from old negroes, haunt me

like swollen tongues unable to speak

so now, I find I am unable to sleep

this is not one of those poems you read

life is just a looking glass

when the season comes around

and you are asked

to spit something profound

I am forced to write these words

the same way nature

forces a snake to shed old skin

the souls of old negroes

forced my hand to write these words

I said I would never write

I speak for those

who have never spoken

I speak for those

who only knew broken English

and were unable to verbalize their thoughts

before I poured my blood on paper

my back bleeds from the sting

of old buffalo whips

because so many refused to conform

so many would rather die

than live in these conditions

refusing new traditions

always speaking without permission

I stand here wishing, just wishing

Walking In My Father's Shoes

you could share

this pain with me - with them

because it will never go away

my ears ache

because the words of fallen spirits

keeps calling me

no matter where I run

they keep following me

this poem will never be read in your classes

but I must get it to the masses

before this year passes

I feel the pain of old negroes in my mind

suspended in the bowels of time

they told me forced apologies

taste like stale wine

so don't bother lying

I have been chosen

to speak for those unable to talk

and I stand for those unable to walk

and I write for those who cannot write

despite what you would like

I spit this poem

for old negro soul's tonight

life is just a looking glass

The Passer By

I saw you

as you passed my way

I choose not a word to say

for you had captured every eye

and I was just the passer by

there are no words to express

how you glide with such finesse

for in one glimpse one thought in time

one phrase, that would not leave my mind

I just looked and choose

not a word to say

proportionately perfect

in every way

so, the next time

you look around and see

that all eyes are looking

as you gracefully glide flawlessly

across the floor

it is the proportionally

Perfection

they all adore

Political Piece

I believe every poet needs

a political piece

where they would take the time to say

or even drop those common clichés'

or to spit some conscious thought at least

yeah... I believe every poet needs

a political piece

we all have pondered the idea

of being able to manipulate time

then we look around and find

something substantial

that plays drums with our minds

we all wish some things would cease and desist

like lawmakers spending too much time

on young lawbreakers

structuring sentences that erases them

forever from our midst

then there are those young boys

with broken wrist

from the pressure of hand cuffs

that don't even fit

I am talking a political piece

life is just a looking glass

that will force everyone to vote

whether they still think it's a game

or treat it the same

that would be one inalienable right

they would quote

then we step to the judge

that believes ghetto love

is dropping 20 year sentences

on fake gangsters

making them terminal thugs

you should know after 400 years

there have been too many tears

and grandmothers spit so much truth

into black youth's young ears

I am not saying that we heard it all

but we do recognize the need to call

for some help

totally aware we are no longer

naked and bare

living life just for self

you see I am talking a political piece

unlike those you may have heard before

the type that after you wipe

Walking In My Father's Shoes

still leaves stains

on your cerebrum's door

then we'd step to the congress and senate

and see so few that look like us

making eyes open to society

letting lies be our sobriety

now we no longer idly fuss

creating new dialog to privately discuss

so there can be new found purpose

birthed in the heart of us

then we venture into the school system

to try and understand those standardized test

if the first test given

was found to be racially biased

and in the evolutionary process

they were under such duress

when they were forced to hire us

now they are teaching a test all year

making it mandatory that our children pass

as we are entering this global race

and education is sat at the Internet's pace

leaving America's urban youth

ranked nearly dead last

life is just a looking glass

now you see how a political piece

began from one perspective

then encompassed us all

read of Greece, Athens,

Rome and other early kingdoms

so chaotic was their fall

I am talking a political piece

Not of how Ford pardoned Nixon

for the crimes he committed

or the popular argument

between the democrats and republicans

on votes that were or were not

counted and submitted

you see I believe every poet needs

a political piece

whether they would take the time to say

or even drop those common clichés'

just to spit some conscious thought at least

yeah,

I believe every poet needs a political piece

On The Seashore

each time I stand by the clear blue ocean

my heart beats with the waves I see

wondering how many heroes

never had a chance to grow

into the person they were meant to be

for no human being could withstand the pressure

of being the lesser - for a full eternity

whether you were considered three fifths or half

while on paper you were supposed to be free

I have visited other shores

seeing places, where angry faces

knew I stood for American liberty

all the time in my mind

I am still struggling to be free

I have always had the notion - that the ocean

was never the proper burial ground

for hundreds of millions of slaves

that refused to go for trade

whose remains still lay on the oceans ground

now you tell me that it's fair

when America still doesn't care

demanding we deserve no reparations

life is just a looking glass

so how can we appeal - if no one wants to heal

or truly repair this tattered nation

I wish there were some words

somewhere you would have heard

that could almost make you understand

just how I feel

if we add the total sum

of all the lost souls - plus this one

you would have no doubt this pain is real

as I stand and watch the waves

where they start and where they fade

I can still hear their spirits singing

how can you still have a song

when this pain is journey's long

and my tears just keep on ringing

as I sit by the oceans floor

although slavery is no more

can we ever right this wrong

it is sad because we know it

but we are all afraid to show it

as we sing those same old songs

will there ever come a day

when freedom will have its way

Walking In My Father's Shoes

as it is written in the declaration

much like a cancer that is banal

justice actually goes on trial

every day throughout this nation

you can see our own governments contradiction

affirmative action results are fiction

highlights all the media's pages

since we've always been the last hired

and the first to be laid off or fired

it has been the same through all the ages

yes, we have had a few promotions

now it's concluded with the notion

all the wrongs have been made right

but as I stand by the oceans shore

I find I don't fear no more

so with every breath I have - I fight

life is just a looking glass

Spilled Ink

I like to hear

others poets

flow

the words the verbs

the things they know

to me

it is just like

spilled ink

some words

you write down

and some

you just think

no matter what you

may have heard

the story

doesn't end

until the last poet

stops and puts down

his pen

Erasing The M's

As children we were always told that "can't" is one word that should be erased from our entire vocabulary. Creating the mindset that we can do whatever we put our minds to. While attending school there were some things our teachers told us were not possible, maybe it was just the times or some other factor that I am unable to grasp at this moment. Everything we are taught has substance, therefore we need to place it in our lesson bank to retract whenever the need arises.

After graduating and completing the requirements for the institutions of higher learning, there were things we found somehow leaned more toward the first lesson of can't than anything else we could recall. Now, I have chosen a new reality, a new way of approaching life's most challenging encounters. I have created a mental eraser with the ability to remove the obstacles that were believed at first glance unmovable. I have erased all the M's whether they began with M or Im; such as, there are no more issues considered to be impossible or improbable. I have erased them all.

Although, this doesn't make reaching or attaining goals or purpose any easier, it does give more power and more effort to the don't quit or don't give up attitude. Failure to me is the ability to try again with enhanced understanding of the matter. I can now see through the

life is just a looking glass

maze and the clutter of mountains and other obstacles standing in my path. If a way around it or through it is not discovered or detected, I always carry the proper tools to begin burrowing my way to the other side. Time then becomes a friend and foe, but not a discouraging factor. No stated impossibility should hinder you from continuing forward. As we look back historically, there were many things before considered truly impossible. Such as flying, the automobile, walking on the moon and a multitude of other discoveries we now consider to be common occurrences.

Now instead of giving up; I put my whole effort into moving forward, no one ever said it would be easy. As a matter of fact, it was stated to be much harder than it really is, but I suppose that was just a verbal deterrent for the week hearted. With no more impossibilities blocking my brain waves and not worrying about the shadows of doubt hovering high above, I will one day reach my appointed place. Pressing ever forward toward the mark of that higher calling, we all have one you know. So, the eternal echo which I have placed in my mind I then turned the volume to the max, it continues to repeat over and over and over, "Giving up is not an option".

Choice

Intelligent decisions...

Intelligent decisions...

I am told this is not one

but I add, the sum of my quality education

my undesired situations

and some considering me not being

an equitable member, in this esteemed population

then I guess

I just be a poet

at least that's what I've been told

I could have chosen some intellectual endeavor

to manipulate what someone else creates

to try and make their creations better

but instead

instead I chose this word thang

creating and spitting my very own slang

and still I'm told I'm playing games

everywhere I go

I look and marvel

at all the beauty, that is yet to be explained

then I hear songs on the radio

and wonder, man

life is just a looking glass

why they choose those words to sang

so instead of saying I choose this

maybe these words I should just dismiss

what if this poetry chose me

what if this poetry chose me

then would I be too blind to see

or merely separated by too many degrees

my blood flows like ink

with every beat of my heart

new phrases and words are created

each time my eyelashes blink

at the very root of my dreads

I was bred to spit what's read

now I be, the very words

that make up this poetry

and if it flows

if it flows like rain

then it be my blood

that stains the pages, here

read my palms

and ask the sages

did I choose - or did it choose

or did we choose together

I am saying

did I choose - or did it choose

or did we choose together

some nights

I wish I didn't have to write

then maybe, just maybe

I could sleep much better

so often I see myself

painted by the tip of my pen

then the night comes and the Sun rises

and it starts all over again

I believe these words are just what I be

if I were hospitalized

for surgery

when they cut me open

all they would see

are the passionate words

of some beautiful soliloquy

you see, I choose this

I choose to sit up most nights

long days and just write

until the blood

no longer flows from my pen

or that I'm on my way to emergency

while having

some epileptic fit

neither will be the case

I'm just practicing

these words I spit

I don't believe you

have ever experienced

true emotional bliss

so I guess, I can never

make you understand

why, **I CHOOSE THIS!**

life is just a looking glass

then I'd have to type

whatever I wanted to write

and that still wouldn't be the end

because I choose this

so many poets died unknown

before any words they had written

were ever seen in print

and you wonder why I think

or why I say, this gift is heaven sent

you see, I choose this

maybe you can't catch me

or you're too blind to see

how these poetic flows

are constantly sustaining me

but you see - I choose this

ok, maybe I could have had a different job

in a different life

and found some different feelings

for an unhappy wife

who thought this poetry shhh was just full of strife

but you see, I choose this

probably one day you'll pass me driving

thinking I must be truly sick

life is just a looking glass

The Declaration of Indecision

here we are

in the land of the free

enjoying the life

of the freedoms that be

walking around believing

we play a true part

not even knowing

where this freedom stuff started

so when you declare

independence

what does it mean?

are you fighting

the powers that be?

or is it just for the King?

have you ever read

the declaration

Jefferson wrote

they excluded us

and all it took

was one note

in the Constitution the word slave

does not appear

Walking In My Father's Shoes

if you were three / fifths of a person

what words would you hear?

no right to vote

no freedom of speech

nowhere to go

no lessons to teach

the words of the Preamble

are echoing our needs

but those words have never

been true to its creed

so when you proclaim

such acts of indecision

made by men of true statue

great men with no vision

who created documents

with such generalities

through time

has been interpreted

to meet our gradual needs

we stand here today

thinking we are truly free

but that can easily be taken

by the powers that be

life is just a looking glass

it's not an invisible foe

as you have heard

or you may think

for we struggle

not against men

but, mere paper and ink

we can be written out

as easily as we were added in

who knows just how far

true freedom transcends

so we must re-write

the few words we treasure

and make them our bond

we hold without measure

for as long as those words

on the Amendments remain

no one can question

how much we have gained

"for we hold the truths to be self-evident, that…"

Redemption
(for Tookie Williams)

I find it strange

always having to convince others

how I feel like Moses

holding all these promises

on my tongue

and sometimes I feel like Job

I never knew so many problems

could actually come

as I sit in this jail without bail

trying to figure out

where the hell I went wrong

my mind replays like church on Sundays

singing some old gospel songs

it's not the origin of where they came from

but rather the message they now send

as I sit in this square unaware

of which me I should defend

I believe we all have alter ego's

living both good and bad

and I know we have all done things

some of we wish we never had

life is just a looking glass

I have found in life, there are only two options

to be or not - right

in turn, there are only two actions

either you quit or you fight

now as I search for cause

or the battles that need to be won

but there are no military battalions

just an army of one

there is no path less taken

your path is the one you set

if you don't believe

your existence is predetermined

you haven't lived just yet

one of the oddest things about people is

no one cares who save them

just as long as they do

even though they may cheat, lie and steal

what they expect from me is the truth

who would believe I choose to live with pride

how will I tell my dog's

I would rather die than ride

it will take all the strength I have to show

I stand in the middle and not on either side

Walking In My Father's Shoes

I've been given a second chance

so I know, I owe something for that

now the time has arrived and I must decide

because I gotta pay something back

I can only teach from this book of life

and the lessons I've been through

in turn I hope you learn from me

this could just as easily happen to you

all it takes is one mistake

hanging out at the right time wrong place

and whatever happens next

can never be erased

even if the apology is sincere

it is impossible to bring someone back

then every day you are locked away

from those you hold dear

it's too hard to live like that

I am trying to get this message out

while I still have breath

so you won't make the same mistakes

and fail the same test

I am here to tell you - death row

ain't no place for a man to go

life is just a looking glass

ain't no place for a man to grow

if you ask me

I've talked to those

who lived there

that's how I know

I have to remember

you may not believe

in the same book

I choose to read

and you may not believe

I am just this farmer sowing seeds

the realest thing

you could ever do

is hold your head high

and open blind eyes

with the lasting words

of the truth

Untitled

we sit and wait

for the perfect time

as we script our lives

in prose and rhyme

sometimes missing

the precious few

every day we live

time dims our view

we can't afford to let

one moment past

we must do our best

at every task

and search for answers

to each question our children ask

and let our smiles

shine through

the pain we mask

no longer searching

for the perfect time

because perfection

is placed in every line

life is just a looking glass

I Pardoned America

I recently I decided to draft

a formal letter to the White House

I truly felt it was time

to get some lifelong burdens

off my chest, the letter began

to the past and present, presidential

and governing legislative bodies

of these United States of America

I, A. J. Houston, on this day

do pardon you

for all past and present atrocities

whether hidden in secret files of the FBI

or written on blacked out pages for all to see

this includes all acts of extreme prejudice

against those of whom this land originally belonged

and those of my ancestors

of whom were legally murdered

for land, invention, or merely used to set an example

for blatant acts of injustice

and malicious acts of prejudice.

I... pardon you

but there are over three hundred million

citizens around the globe

awaiting a sincere I'm sorry

maybe I saw it first in a dream

or read it somewhere in the unwritten book

of "The Art of Peace"

one of the first steps must be

if two men are found to disagree

one must then offer a true apology

so… I apologize

for all the lies, all the spies

for this society's slowly but constant demise

and to think this is the land of freedom and liberty

or is it just an illusion

while those of color, are blinded by

a life of governmental exclusion

for such tragic capers

the offer of green paper, could never suffice

for more than four centuries of pain

with no one to shoulder the blame

what value do you place

on just one, innocent life

I offer this apology to you

life is just a looking glass

Because, that's what real men do

I can no longer blame the man

for if I be a man

living in this land, if I had but one leg

on that leg I'd stand

in this America the beautiful

in this home of the free

America have found a way for centuries

to not include me

from those lost in the passage

to those hung from trees

we've spent more than four lifetimes

begging on our knees

for just a glimpse at some freedom

and a chance at equality

so, I can either use this time, or lose my mind

but I chose to offer this apology

I have found myself apologizing

for the terrorizing

of the Indians, the Mexicans,

the slaves, and presently the Blacks

if my apology be true

I must also pardon you

for the night flames, the slanderous names

the drugs and the gats

I pardon you for not making it

a constitutional amendment

after years of residency

it is still possible to see

The Voting Rights Act rescinded

and for those families with no medical insurance

and those without enough food, to feed their young

before they go to bed

to those veterans

who fought for freedom

and have no place to lay their heads

and to those schools lacking

revenue for free lunches

and equitable funds to pay those who teach

and to we the other people

who always find equality

just beyond our reach

I needed to write this formal letter

to pardon you

to get these burdens off my chest

but there are so many things I left out

life is just a looking glass

Word Warrior

"Poets... ATTENTION! Parade... REST"

I am a student of the perfection of war

I choose to battle with words

because evil thoughts are such formidable foes

I lay concepts, like land mines on poetic battle grounds

the art of creating must have been beautiful

when a poem truly meant something

now it seems, we be but Gazelles in the den of Lions

as we dance with no purpose, on stages with no sound

I am but a soldier in this perfection of war

practicing the martial arts of piercing words

how can I find time to raise souls from the past

and breathe new life into verse

I wish I could have seen Langston, in his days of glory

where words forged bonds beyond continents of history

at an early age my father taught me to take

Two thirds of words, and half of a whole to create meaning

because there are only two things

I should ever be afraid of

Zig Zag lightning, and the wrath of God

and no man be an equal to either

Walking In My Father's Shoes

my how I wish, I could have

stood on the peaks of the Himalayas

when God spoke words of the thunder

splitting night and day in two

and marveled as the storms

ceased to rage at the phrase "Peace be still"

all should know

thoughts are such formidable foes

and words the ultimate weapon

I have seen words walk ocean tops

but have yet to see them fly

tonight my only purpose

is to feel them rise high

far past the galaxies unknown - rise

higher surpassing musical tones - rise

so that I may join the ranks

of ancient word warriors

who have sacrificed life for truth

in these murky waters of shame and blame

what words do we leave for our youth

I have traveled far, and met many who write

but so few whose words, were beacons of light

you can live a life filled with wishes and hope

life is just a looking glass

but no war can be fought with just jesters and jokes

so tell me, why be there wars

if not to preserve the truths we write

why does gravity always prevail

when sadness fails

to let our words take flight

leaders once lead by example

and a poet was measured

by the words they say

now our leaders lie

to get the votes of the people

and poets are ranked

by the jokes they display

no matter how much truth you write

or how much pain is placed in your verse

when you think you got it bad

stop and look around you

because someone else has got it worse

I am just a student

in the perfection of war

I choose to battle with words

If it be possible to awaken

dead minds from mere rhetoric

More

sometimes

I would rather hold the book

than to read it

it's weight, it's sure weight

reminds so much of those thoughts

that are so heavy

I have yet to write them down

Sometimes

it becomes incomprehensible

that life can be forged by vowels

often misspoken by those with less intent

forgotten moments, can never by captured

Simply by displaying great penmanship

for writing, that real writing

starts in the soul of thought

it can never be sold or bought

there is no way to control what's sought

it must first, surge through your veins

like the blood that flows

through your heart to your brain

enabling you to conjure

ideas that smells of ancient wonder

ideas no man can put asunder

making lightning and thunder

sit in timeless moments waiting

waiting for you, to thank all those

who scribed life before you

leaving pages describing all the ages

showing you the door to

enlightenment, so the excitement

can take you and make you -be more to

Because that's what I want to be

MORE

you know? More than just a sayer of words

I want to do more than hold the page

and stand on the stage, for my voice to be heard

so often, it is those concepts you write

that makes you more than you are

it's those thoughts forged into space

that makes you look in the face

of past failures ugly scars

but sometimes

I want to hold the page, so I can see it

and sometimes, I want to close my eyes

recite the poem, to see if I can be it

this year, I have already

written up my plan for improvement

I have already set a date

to stand hand in hand with fate

so I can finally clean the slate

I need to get past all those times

I was too afraid to try

thinking it was so much better

to just live safe and die

hiding in the comfortable shade I had made

satisfied with just getting by

now every group of children I work with

every time I hold a creative writing workshop

every time I pick up my pen

I want to write the words, that mean more

I want to spit verbal wings

that rise up and brings

your left and right brain

to levels of consciousness

so much higher than ever before

I am not looking to be, the best poet you see

it's these words I want you to adore

because all I ever aspire to be is... **MORE**

life is just a looking glass

Passion For Pain

I find every writer of poetry

must first possess, a passion for pain

no field of study could prepare your soul

for the nakedness

of bare all truth, found in the murky trenches

of a poet's mind

sometimes I feel those that hear me

know me better, than I know myself

we tend to shield ourselves

from the cold hard facts of our lives

hiding them on pages for all to see

I've lost friends and family in this wicked society

when you read it in my verse

the pain is there, the hurt is there

but no names appear

so you may think, it a normal passing day

I have had love to vanish

while held in the clutches of my heart

that hurt so bad

even my pen cries as I scribe moments

never to be dimmed by the passing of time

Walking In My Father's Shoes

desperately struggling to make

a living at these words

often I would feel

better served with a sign

on the street corner

of song and dance

unwilling to reveal

I dance to no music, no joy

just the recent tragedy of yesterdays

grasping old thoughts curled into new corners

refusing to step into the light

praying they remain out of sight

hoping not to disclose all of this time

I know I possess a passion for pain

if you follow the lines of my verse

to the blood I shed writing them

you can still see wounds - open

dripping my life's essence

on cold white slabs of paper

and I the mortician

painstakingly dressed them up nicely

so you could never witness

the morbid scenes of truth

life is just a looking glass

old poems reveal, as just another conjured lie

I grimace through smiling teeth

as I give life to another poem

so you would never know, I must do this

I gotta say this - my mind could burst into flames

if I don't snatch these gray thoughts

from my brain, darkened by pain

stained by yesterday's long since forgotten

sometimes I bleed words so bare

I struggle not to notice

the sound of laughter only shared

when there is too much remorse to cry

I believe all poets

must have a certain tolerance for pain

because real life, is never funny to those living it

when I show you what is seen

through my mind's eye

it is impossible to write in joke form

time is like a silent movie

no enemy music to warn you

of the horrors of this life

no cutting from the scene

before new dreams are beheaded

Walking In My Father's Shoes

I don't believe one can merely

use their imagination

to skillfully scribe

such pain experienced

only in the after birth of life

every sleepless night

I rest my head on a stack

of battered poetry books

stuffed so full with passion

the pages are afraid to touch

from the terror of spilling

already dried blood

I labor daily

with these alphabetic concoctions

attempting to become a true alchemist

transforming indigestible pain

into a palatable intake

because when I share it

I can't take it back

please, take it with you

that be just one day's load of burdens

and now

I must prepare for tomorrow

life is just a looking glass

True Love

I've been practicing for eternity

because today I choose

to write your name across the heavens

etch your face into the clouds

and on every sunset

so everyone who looks

up regardless of the season

would wish they were me

I am asked on a continued basis

where do I hide my genie?

Where do I keep my magic lamp?

I must have used at least

three wishes, for your smile

I have finally figured it out

you must have been created

the day after God rested

it is a scientific anomaly

one person can contain

so much beauty inside and out

every time you sleep

the planets become motionless

Walking In My Father's Shoes

waiting to impress you

with circular cycles of excitement

each time your eyes open

I have become life's true optimist

I am flattered by life's challenges

so I am forced to write words like this

now everyone can look up

and know what they've missed

I remember the day, the earth stood still

anticipating the moment, for you to arrive

I have seen the moon glow through a total eclipse

just to embrace your face

I put all my prayers on speed dial

because I have no time to waste

you possess the sweetest nectar

any man could ever taste

you ask me

if my love comes with a forever guarantee

I promise, from this day forward

to give you every piece of me

for even you know throughout all of time

love has never been pain free

I'll offer you my breath, if you need more security

life is just a looking glass

I find myself counting rain drops

between thoughts of you, until the rain stops

you are the only one I know

with your smile can make a rainbow

before the rains come and go

I snatched up all the love

I've ever given in the past

to add to this relationship

to make this one last

just yesterday - I erased all my memories

now, my every thought is you

I could write every day for a lifetime

and still have words never to measure up

unable to say enough

leaving out all the good stuff

so, with my paper and pen, I spend

all my time, struggling to find

metaphors to define you

so the whole world will know

and history will show

I've spent every day

doing my best

to love you too

Why Me

my father, had a tracheotomy

unable to talk

only speaking with the aid of batteries

cancer in the throat

from smoking too many cigarettes

and here I am

I am not a chain smoker, but I can't quit

standing here a bonafied nicotine addict

every day promising myself, I won't be like my dad

riding the train to pain

thinking, hoping, it won't be me

chemo, one lung,

praying it won't spread to my legs or my heart

if it wasn't for that billion-dollar lawsuit

television and movies

would still display it as being cute

every actor, whether or not they smoked

holding a burning cigarette

I don't know if I have nicotine

in my brain or in my veins

no matter where it is, it's all the same

one cigarette left

life is just a looking glass

promising myself - this time, I'll quit

none of that nicorette or hypnotic shhh

cold turkey this time

so I'll just buy one more pack

just in case I change my mind

at best, I am smoking more

and enjoying it less

every time I see a red light

or smoke coming from a

nearby automobile exhaust

I gotta fire one up

I can taste it on my breath

see it on my lips

wearing nicotine on my teeth

why me, why me

that is probably the same words

used by my father

although, they never appeared

in any of his movements

long after surgery

you could still see him, put fire to his addiction

blowing clouds of life

with each painful exhaust

and I still can't stop

what manner of demons, come twenty in a pack

with each purchase, I hear the sound

of whips on flesh

as my ancestors were forced

to work tobacco fields

helping corporations to make another billion

and I am still supporting slavery

no matter how minute

donating dollars, I don't have

for the continued destruction, of human life

why me

I hear myself say it everyday

as my lips grow darker

I've convinced myself, cold turkey - cold turkey

is only eaten, the day after thanksgiving

I can't stop

so I dig so much deeper than before

to find enough change, to buy another pack

six dollars now, and I can't afford it

although making a concerted effort

I can't ignore it

in my poetic eulogy for the dying

life is just a looking glass

I can't stop crying

and I'll never stop trying, to quit

why me

if I tell you I care

and I don't want you inhaling

my second hand smoke

but I can't stop

so to you empty words

fall like some sick joke

whether sunshine, rain or freezing cold

left standing outside

it is illegal now to burn one in most buildings

now it is considered suicide

as I consume this dark matter

it must not matter

every young person I see

I try and convince them to quit

while they still believe, it is just for fun

because suicide, is so much quicker

when your poison is a bullet

Instead of two black lungs

Why Me?

The Voices of Angels

(opening short)

we spend our lives

craving just a taste of LOVE

I refuse to believe

my thirst, for this truth in verse

is simply a waste of blood

I hope when these word hit you

you will treat them like scriptures

and let your thoughts

flow like floods

no matter what you think

this poem is not written in ink

but formed in the sky above

The Voices Of Angels

life is just a looking glass

The Voices of Angels

I've been writing poetry all of my life

but recently I had to stop

for the last four months

I've been on a quest, to find love

you know, that still feels like

the beginning kind of love

that always and forever never ending, kind of love

I just needed to feel what I felt

when I first started writing

I didn't write for performance, or for slams

if no one ever read it

I was satisfied by just writing it

now I practicing writing backwards

trying to find that adoration

for the alphabets, all over again

before any words are formed

before any concepts can be attached

it's strange how sometimes our dreams

are able to reveal our true purpose

I only say this, because the other night in a dream

Langston, David the Psalmist, William

and all those others, I've always held in great esteem

they sat around my bed

and told me, what moved me

was their spirits soaring through me

and these words, were the only thing to soothe me

then said, I was the source of inspiration

for everything, they ever wrote

Einstein told me this thing about time

He said, time is not linear like we believe it to be

it exists in the past, the present

and the future simultaneously

now I can say with true conviction

I am the one, who lights up the sun

giving you the illusion of day

darkness is also my responsibility

so I split the dark from the light

which made the night - that's when I write

water was the hardest thing to create

it is the sustainer of life in humans

and every creature, in the oceans, ponds and lakes

it would have been tragic

if there was just the simplest mistake

I know I am not the only one, who's taken the time

to measure the exact distance

life is just a looking glass

between right and wrong

took the metric meter, added lines to it

called it a measurement

so singers could sing their songs to it

this writing, you still wonder why I do it

I knew there was something special about me early in life

because in grade school, my teachers

loved everything I wrote

but I held my pen so tight

and used such force, at each deliberate stroke

that one my teacher told me

"I needed to change the way I held my pen"

I wish what I know now

I would have known back then

I should have asked her, shouldn't it depend

if I draw these words from the depths of my mind

or does God place them in my hands

I no longer need to copyright any of my words

I have four of the greatest

scientific minds on loan

and I am authorized at anytime

to contact them by phone

no matter how hard I've tried

it is impossible, to un-write this poem

so those who bite it

can on taste it, in its molecular form

I finally gathered enough strength

to take every negative thing through this life

that has ever been said to me

script it in this book of pain

so every night its read to me

regurgitated all the lies

this society's ever feed to me

and I cut my wrist

now all that exist

is this truth in verse

that is bleed from me

the other night

I like Jacob, wrestled with an angel all night

until he loaned me this verse

he told me, in order for you to comprehend it

I had to stop and comprehend it first

right after Langston and William said to me

"They only wrote, what they wrote

because that's what they heard from me"

I woke up, washed my face

life is just a looking glass

saw they had left this tattoo

that read POET on my tongue

so I bowed my head

and asked God why?

and his reply

the truth...

always begins, with ONE!

I've been writing poetry all my life

for constant hours I rehearse

but every time you see me on this mic

my whole life - is in this verse

Purpose

I can remember back in the day

I did so many things

growing up, I played so many roles

and as you may know

finding your true purpose

really takes a toll, on one's soul

I guess the last thing I can recall

I wanted to be an actor / singer

but that was just a stepping stone

before I made these words my life

now poetry is my home

I've tried behind the camera

in front of the camera

beside the camera

but my place, is on this stage

hell nah!

I ain't got no attitude problem

I let the ink spill my rage

if you want Shakespeare

I'll become the sonnet

if you want Keats

I'll be the best written prose

life is just a looking glass

in these words I thought up

I'm so caught up

I'm like a junkie

I'll snort these words up my nose

no-one in here can refute

this world has no substitute

for that one thing you wrote

that one thought you created

that takes your breath

and leaves you powerless

for time could never date it

we are all mere humans

locked in this cocoon

of life ending too soon

acting like cowboys

thinking like penslingers at high noon

have you ever noticed how

some people pick up a pen, like a habit

while others treat their pen like a job

but to me this writing never ends

because the way I hold my pen

you would think I was the mob

slanging ink like paint

you can sit there all night

with a brand new pen

and new feelings to write

but the thoughts you're thinking

I've already thanked?

yeah - thanked

so if you're sitting there held captive

like I am some kind of magician

don't feel ashamed, it ain't no game

I am a true technician

I build words like the pyramids

I make foundations out of paper

I'll lock your mind up, like Ft. Knox

your thoughts couldn't be any safer

I have learned to write

staying up late at night

delving into places no one else has been

giving imagination life, giving logic to strife

giving heartache a true friend

I am no longer searching for purpose

I have already surpassed my goals

for if I am performing this poem

at this slam tonight

life is just a looking glass

it is you that feeds my soul

but sometimes

I aspire to inspire myself

damn...

when I read the words I write

I often inquire

because I would even hire myself

as a ghost writer to write

the thoughts between the thoughts

I didn't have enough time to get to

if I had two of me

maybe then I could be

exactly what I was meant to

I hang out with inspiration

we be chill'n like brothers on a quest

the only bad thing, is inspiration can't sing

and he only shows up late at night

so I can't get no rest

hold up! Sssshh - did you here that?

I think I hear my pen calling

I guess that would be a sight

but before I go, I want you to know

(sigh) this is the best night of my life

Walking In My Father's Shoes

Things Father's Need To Tell Their Son's

Before They Become Father's

I speak in my grandfather's voice

his name tattooed across my chest

he departed this existence

to make room for my arrival

no one ever said I stand in his resemblance

my mirror smiles back a sign of acknowledgment

sons are just their father's clones

wrapped tightly in different skin

I prayed my lessons would embed themselves

in their chakra's

not all prayers are answered in time

some may lay restful in the bed of sound

in which they were created

but know this of life

there is only one chance to get it right

time will present multiple options

take more than one moment to make your choice

and contrary to the beliefs of others

it is never too late to change your direction

un believers will surround you - it's their purpose

life is just a looking glass

there can be no testimony

without a test of your resolve

keep your head high in order to see clearly

the surface in front of you

look back only to remember

how far you've traveled from humble beginnings

my father stood proud

until he could stand no more

you are a direct descendant of him

practice the placement of your feet

the direction you point your toes matters

walk in honor and remembrance

I saved these branches

it is all I could locate of our family tree

think not of it idly

plant in fertile ground and use water

to construct your own

there is so much we don't know of love

voids in our genealogical make up

lost parts of our history in fields of plowed cotton

covered our lips with silence

to hush the jingling of chains

the strongest men were forced from their families

Walking In My Father's Shoes

to build this country on which we stand

I sketched for you a diagram

of the weakest points on this body

only to find they are different on each model

do not be afraid to cover your eyes

when beauty attacks you

at the core of your being

there's this thing called a first mind

follow it if you have the strength

for heaven knows it is not easy

love is a locked and loaded full clip

with one round chambered in an Uzi

it will seldom miss when you pull the trigger

keep the safety in the on position

it has been noted and sang in songs for years

all is fair in love and war

so take the time needed to zero your weapon

it increases your ability to hit the target

the legs of men are weak

falling too easily when tripped up

learn to keep your balance

we were once tight roped promise walkers

it's alright to fall

life is just a looking glass

be more careful where you land

we love full throttle

a dual holly four barreled carburetor

with a 357 engine on a tricycle

running too fast to catch up with ourselves

slow down

I learned by trial and error

often more error than trial

you will judge yourself more harshly

find leniency in your own court of opinion

there is a great story of old

where removing one rib was enough

to create the perfect mate

interpret how you must

but know this of women

their smiles are worth their weight in riches

do not enthrall your self

in the chiseled structure in which she glides

there is more beauty underneath

the layers of seduction than you can ever imagine

show her your teeth

there's a certain elegance

in displaying the real you

when captured by sound

remove your mask

let her see truth glisten

in the pupils of your eyes

each day is a gift

so have the presence of mind

to give thanks

for safe keeping

hide this under your tongue

followers never fit

the shoes they are wearing

they belong to someone else

BE YOUR OWN MAN!

you are a chosen replica

of my father's father

family crest across your mane

falling is as intricate apart of walking

as failure closely mimics success

you will befriend them both

be not afraid

for you have my blood

coursing through your heart

trouble is your distant cousin

life is just a looking glass

do not hang out

with him too much

you possess

all you need to make it

and never forget

pray before and after

each and every step you take

I am not requiring you

to believe wholeheartedly

I have faith enough

for all of us

work proves itself

while on the other hand

words, well

words need work

-aj houston-

life is just a looking glass

Additional Products by AJ Houston

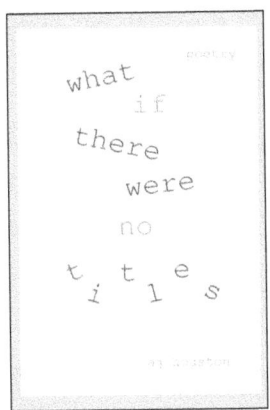

New Titles Coming Soon
Not Yet Lost Jan 2016
F.A.C.E. June 2016
(Fibromyalgia Awareness Changes Everything)
The Legend of Shrenk July 2016
Lost Pens
(A Pocket Guide for Writers)

all books can be purchased @ amazon.com, createspace, or at the next performance to receive a personalized signature. Booking and contact information can be located on the last page of this book.

Acknowledgements

I have learned to appreciate everyone I have ever come in contact with for their donation, whether it be positive or negative the input was of value. I am grateful for all who added love or subtracted love, making me aware there is so much love inside each of us. I Thank everyone which means there would be too many names to place in such a small space. Especially my Father to whom this book is dedicated, may he rest in peace. Thank You.

life is just a looking glass

Author's Bio

A.J. Houston, born Albert Jeffrey Houston in Dallas, Texas. Began writing at an early age from the motivation he garnered from his favorite author, Dr. Seuss. If you would ask him why he writes, he would laugh and probably quote a line from "Green Eggs and Ham", "I am Sam, Sam I am". In his workshops, he teaches "Green Eggs and Ham" is a book mirroring the American ideology of color.

There are so many nuances to discover in the grouping of words. His belief and practice that pens are merely paint brushes of a singular color, able to present pictures disguised as alphabets. He is the founder of Not Just Alphabets; created in 1999, a company built of everything you can do with words and sound. Teaching creative writing to all ages, along with performance workshops. The purpose of the classes is to use poetry and writing as emotional release and a healing process. Using pens and pencils can be fun and an exciting exercise for the fingers of young boys and girls alike. Poetry has proven valuable for use in battered women shelters, prisons, youth detention centers, alternative schools and with youth from elementary to high school. The structure of lessons offered in higher level institutions differ in scope, to include essays, oral presentations, and enhance the overall skill of writing a clear and precise paper.

Writing is his life. His goal is to produce books with lasting concepts and timeless verses. A.J. Houston, is a proud father and grandfather, he believes writing is the perfect anecdote to discovering the innermost feelings and the true way to evaluate oneself. His mantra is: "In preparing for tomorrow, you must first acknowledge, this day was the tomorrow you spoke of yesterday... being or becoming your best, isn't an accident, you have to attain the skills necessary and become your best on PURPOSE".

Contact Information:

njalphabets.org

www.twitter.com/ajwordartist

www.facebook.com/ajhouston

www.youtube.com/ajhouston

www.reverbnation.com/ajhouston

ajwordartist@gmail.com

instagram.com/ajwordartist

periscope.com/ajwordartist

Additional Products:

CD 's   Love Seasons - The Awakening - Whispers

Books Coming Soon

The Legend of Shrenk

Not Yet Lost

F. A. C. E.
(Fibromyalgia Awareness Changes Everything)

Lost Pens
(A Pocket Guide For Writers)

T-Shirts

Poetic Lessons

NJA Gear

For Booking: **Contact**

AJ Houston

@ **poetajhouston@gmail.com**

Thank you for your support

Thank you for your support:

Our goal is to create products we are Proud to present. Please feel free to use the contact information to let us know what you think of the products we offer and also for booking tours and events. We believe in the power of words. Peace and Blessings.

www.ingramcontent.com/pod-product-compliance
Lightning Source LLC
Chambersburg PA
CBHW051103160426
43193CB00010B/1298